# RESILIENT LIFE

## LIFE

JOURNAL AND PLANNER

## A DAILY GUIDE TO STRENGTH, HOPE, AND MEANING

NAME _____

EMAIL _____

PHONE _____

DATE _____

ZONDERVAN
BOOKS

ZONDERVAN BOOKS

*Resilient Life Journal and Planner*
Copyright © 2023 by Rebekah Lyons

Requests for information should be addressed to:
Zondervan, *3900 Sparks Dr. SE, Grand Rapids, Michigan 49546*

Zondervan titles may be purchased in bulk for educational, business, fundraising, or sales promotional use. For information, please email SpecialMarkets@Zondervan.com.

ISBN 978-0-310-36543-3 (hardcover)

Author is represented by Meredith Brock at The Brock Agency.

*Cover design: Riley Moody*
*Cover illustration: Hannah Joiner Crosby*
*Interior design: Aaron Campbell and Denise Froehlich*

*Printed in India*

23 24 25 26 27 28 29 /REP/ 10 9 8 7 6 5 4 3 2 1

# WELCOME

Hello Friend,

I'm thrilled to introduce the *Resilient Life Journal and Planner*. This guide is designed to be a companion in your journey to building a more resilient life.

I wish building resilience were a one-and-done thing, that we only needed to pick up and move on after we experience trials, setbacks, or difficulties. But the character of resilience is something altogether different. It's about *becoming* people of resilience, and that *becoming* takes time and practice.

My book *Building a Resilient Life* articulates the five rules of resilience that will help you practice building your emotional and physical strength:

NAME THE PAIN

SHIFT THE NARRATIVE

EMBRACE ADVERSITY

MAKE MEANING

ENDURE TOGETHER

This journal and planner is designed as a guided framework to help you work through these five rules and make their application your own. As you get going, you'll discover what works best for you.

As you build a resilient life, may you experience the strength, hope, and meaning we can achieve only as we face adversity.

Let's begin together!

Rebekah

For further resources on your journey, visit www.RebekahLyons.com.

*Resilience is a daily, consecrated act of remembering
there is something far greater than our present troubles,
which offers us the power to endure and emerge.*

—REBEKAH LYONS

# CONTENTS

* Calendars, Scriptures, Practices, Examines, and Reviews are interspersed in a monthly format beginning on page 36.

# RESILIENCE METHOD

## HOW TO USE THE *RESILIENT LIFE JOURNAL AND PLANNER*

### EXAMINE YOUR OVERWHELM

The first step toward building a resilient life is to assess the state of your own life. You'll begin by furthering your understanding on what resilience is and what it is not. Then you will journey through a series of guided questions to help you examine overwhelm in your life. These questions are intended to help you name areas of pain and shame that are difficult and yet necessary to identify in order to move forward and grow in resilience.

### RESILIENT PRACTICES LIST

These activities are designed to provide you with inspiration as you plan both your monthly calendar and your weekly resilience practices. I encourage you to get creative and include your own ideas in these lists. This section will serve as a resource to return to for ideas throughout your resilience journey.

### MONTHLY CALENDAR

Each month, you'll give your focus to a new rule of resilience. At the start of the month, you'll consider your top priorities in regard to that specific rule, along with your resilience goals for the month. You'll also plan, with intention, activities that will help you build resilience training into your daily, weekly, and monthly schedule.

## SCRIPTURE

At the beginning of each month, you'll find Scripture pages dedicated to that month's rule of resilience. These Scriptures will encourage you and build your faith; they are perfect to meditate on to help you renew your mind in that specific area. You can select from these Scriptures for your weekly Scripture focus.

## PRACTICE

The weekly practice pages are designed to help you establish direction for your week, ensuring you are planning with intention and building the resilient life you desire. Each week, you'll identify a goal, choose an intention to act on, select a Scripture to meditate on, and specify something for which you're grateful. You'll also pinpoint your resilience practices for the week from the included selections (you can also incorporate your own ideas or return to the practices lists on pages 29–33 for more ideas). You'll find that some weeks and some rules may allow for several weekly selections, while others may dictate fewer selections and more focus.

## EXAMINE

Growing in strength, hope, and meaning requires us to make time for introspection and reflection. Each week, you'll be provided with three journal prompts that align with the focus of that month's rule of resilience. These questions will help you examine and assess. This is your space to quiet your soul, listen to God, and grow in vulnerability. These journaling pages will help you understand yourself better and give insight into ways you can further your resilience journey.

## WEEKLY REVIEW

Before you move on to the next week, it's important to take time to review your progress. These pages are intended to help you take note of how the previous week went, to celebrate growing as you go, and to give thought to your intention for the coming week. The review pages are perfect for your weekend practice.

## MONTHLY REVIEW

Upon the completion of each month, take time to review your progress. The monthly review pages give you space to take inventory in real time and reflect on your success in incorporating that month's rule into your everyday life. Take time to acknowledge your growth and set a goal for the coming month.

## RESILIENCE REVIEW

Congratulations! Your commitment to naming the pain, shifting the narrative, embracing adversity, making meaning, and enduring together has helped you become more resilient. In these last pages, take time to look back at the past few months and contemplate your journey—the ups and downs, as well as the achievements. Acknowledge your specific growth and how your plan will help you build a life of resilience.

# BECOMING RESILIENT

## WHAT RESILIENCE IS, AND WHAT IT IS NOT

**Resilience is** our consecrated and daily act of remembering there is something far greater than our present troubles, great or small, and that consecration and remembering give us the power to endure and emerge.

**Resilience is not** an unyielding willpower that pushes through any obstacle. Instead, resilience allows us to be flexible and adaptable. Resilience not only bends but also receives permission to bow out before it breaks. Resilience knows when it's time to stop. There are some storms we must bend low to endure, and there are some storms we must get as far away from as we can. A resilient mind knows the difference.

Resilience is not about sheer strength, and it's not about stubborn persistence either. Resilience is faithful perseverance.

Resilience is not naive optimism either. Resilience is contentment in the acceptance of what *is*.

A life of resilience is one that weathers every storm. It's a life that's nimble, that's surrendered, that's able to imagine new dreams when old dreams die. It's a life that remembers God's promise that he will be with us, even to the end of the age. It's a life that believes that Christ has truly overcome the world.

# EXAMINE YOUR OVERWHELM

*"In this world you will have trouble. But take heart! I have overcome the world."*
—JOHN 16:33

## AMBIGUOUS LOSS

We live in a new age, one in which most of us have suffered a great deal of ambiguous loss. In *Building a Resilient Life*, Rebekah describes ambiguous loss, a term coined by Dr. Pauline Boss, as having no sense of resolution or closure. Doesn't this describe many forms of loss? It's the loss you feel when your expectations don't quite work out, when your kids make decisions you didn't expect, when unexpected circumstances change your plans or divert your dreams. It's the loss of a dream, a sense of purpose, and hope when finances unexpectedly change. It's the loss of whatever you once considered "normal."

Let's take the time to identify our loss.

Have you experienced a loss that has left you without resolution or closure—whether the loss is physical or psychological? Perhaps a divorce, the loss of someone or something you loved, a child moving out of the house, a loved one with Alzheimer's disease or an addiction, a long-distance move, a friendship shifting, a church changing. What is different in your life today than it was a few years ago? What specifically are you grieving?

If you had to describe your loss with feelings, what feelings would you use? Anger, sadness, confusion, discouragement, resentment, guilt, fear?

Many times, in dealing with the pressures of life, we turn to unhealthy coping mechanisms in an effort to numb ourselves to the stress and pain of reality. Do you find yourself turning to alcohol or pills, to work or performance, to entertainment, social media, or shopping? Be honest with yourself and identify all unhealthy coping mechanisms in your life.

Would you consider yourself a resilient person? Why or why not?

Remember, resilience is not an unyielding willpower that pushes through any obstacle. Instead, resilience allows us to be flexible and adaptable. Resilience not only bends but also receives permission to bow out before it breaks.

How are you learning to bend?

What storms have you had to endure?

Where might you need to bow out? What storm do you need to retreat from?

> Resilience isn't about sheer strength, and it's not about stubborn persistence either. Resilience is faithful perseverance.

Do you find yourself operating in persistence or perseverance?

> Resilience is not naive optimism either. Resilience is contentment in the acceptance of what *is*.

On a scale of 1 to 10, how content do you find yourself currently? Do you struggle to accept your circumstances and be content?

## TWO TYPES OF ADVERSITY

*Adversity cultivates resilience.*

There are two kinds of adversity. There's the adversity we can't control, the adversity that is unexpected—a health scare, a marriage upended, a child in crisis—and there's the adversity we take on voluntarily, such as growing a family, shifting careers, or moving across the country.

What adversities in your life have been outside of your control?

.   .   .   .   .   .   .   .   .   .   .   .   .   .   .   .   .   .   .   .   .
.   .   .   .   .   .   .   .   .   .   .   .   .   .   .   .   .   .   .   .   .
.   .   .   .   .   .   .   .   .   .   .   .   .   .   .   .   .   .   .   .   .
.   .   .   .   .   .   .   .   .   .   .   .   .   .   .   .   .   .   .   .   .

What adversities have been voluntary?

.   .   .   .   .   .   .   .   .   .   .   .   .   .   .   .   .   .   .   .   .
.   .   .   .   .   .   .   .   .   .   .   .   .   .   .   .   .   .   .   .   .
.   .   .   .   .   .   .   .   .   .   .   .   .   .   .   .   .   .   .   .   .
.   .   .   .   .   .   .   .   .   .   .   .   .   .   .   .   .   .   .   .   .

Adversity awakens the very thing that trains us toward a more resilient life. When we endure adversity with positivity, curiosity, and reliance on God and community, we develop great resilience.

Can you recall a season of adversity in your life that made you stronger? Describe how you navigated that season and how you grew in strength and resilience.

.   .   .   .   .   .   .   .   .   .   .   .   .   .   .   .   .   .   .   .   .
.   .   .   .   .   .   .   .   .   .   .   .   .   .   .   .   .   .   .   .   .
.   .   .   .   .   .   .   .   .   .   .   .   .   .   .   .   .   .   .   .   .
.   .   .   .   .   .   .   .   .   .   .   .   .   .   .   .   .   .   .   .   .
.   .   .   .   .   .   .   .   .   .   .   .   .   .   .   .   .   .   .   .   .

Here are a list and explanations of the five rules of resilience. If you've read *Building a Resilient Life*, this content will be familiar to you (and I do recommend using the book along with this journal and planner). If you don't have the book or just need a good overview, this section provides some detail about each rule and how you can best live it out.

# THE
# RULES
## of
# RESILIENCE

# Rule One | Name the Pain: *Be Honest*

If we're going to be people who pursue resilience, people who can withstand the chaos of the world, then we have to first deal with our sickness. And how do we identify the sickness? We ask ourselves, *Where does it hurt?*

Rule One helps us understand how recognizing our sin and shame, confessing it to others, and inviting others into our lives can help bring healing.

## Recognize the Shame

The lie of shame whispers, "There is something inherently wrong with you." *You're not enough and never will be*, shame says, so you exhaust yourself trying to prove otherwise. Shame is rooted in your past to remind you of when your best efforts failed; it taunts in your present, pushing you to try harder; and it threatens that you'll fall short in the future. Shame leaves you with a sense of being trapped and powerless, with no agency to change.

## Get Honest and Invite Others In

It's important to practice inviting others in. I had to first be raw and real before God, and then I simply made a commitment to be both honest and honoring of others in my response if someone asked how I was. I would no longer look away and choke out the word "Fine" or, worse, "Great!" when I could offer a truer, more vulnerable response. I made it my aim to make eye contact with integrity, ensuring that my inner life matched my outer life, and give others the safety to do the same. The more I practiced inviting others in, the more they in turn invited me in.

## The Connection between Empathy and Resilience

Empathy breeds connection. When you put yourself in someone else's shoes, you are able to both hear their story more clearly and connect your story with theirs. This shared vulnerability forges connection and offers insights into the life experiences of both of you. Engaging in empathy brings so many benefits because we were made for presence and companionship.

## How God Models Withness

We weren't made to suffer alone. When we share our pain with friends or family members who commit to walk with us through our dark seasons, a shift happens. We're able to walk another mile, make it another day. It allows us to move from surviving to thriving in our everyday lives.

When we receive empathy, we exercise parts of our brain that make us stronger, more emotionally healthy, and better able to withstand the difficulties of life. And when we intentionally engage in empathetic exchange, we become more like God, the creator of withness. In these ways, we ultimately become stronger and better equipped to withstand life's storms. This is how we become more resilient.

## Engage in the Rhythm of Confession

Through confession and forgiveness, we begin to rebuild the pathways of connection and intimacy with people. It's these pathways of intimacy that bring freedom from so much brokenness and shame—the kind of freedom that is crucial to living a resilient life in a resilient community.

# Rule Two | Shift the Narrative: *Renew Your Mind*

Our narrative—the stories we tell ourselves about our lives—becomes a powerful influence on how our minds perceive each moment, and it informs how we respond. If we're going to be people of resilience, it's important to recognize the narratives we tell ourselves, particularly those that are untrue. And when those false narratives raise their ugly heads, people of resilience shift the narrative and speak the truth.

Rule Two teaches us how we can grow stronger each day by preaching to ourselves, retraining our brains, and knowing the truth that sets us free.

## Renew Your Mind and Preach to Yourself

The Bible says that in order to renew our minds we need to fill our thoughts, not just passively observe them. Renewing our minds requires getting serious about the thoughts we have, the books we read, the content we let in, and the ideas we come to trust. We must become vigilant about how we think, what we think, and which inputs we allow in and which ones we throw out. A resilient life can be built by taking account of our thoughts—what we are letting in and what we are putting out—but it will take getting serious about retraining our brains to think differently.

Preaching to ourselves requires the knowledge of what is actually true, the security that our identity comes from Christ, and the wisdom to discern when toxic thinking invades our mental space. We must press into the continuous invitation to believe that God is faithful to complete what he begins. And then we must preach that truth to ourselves daily. If we do, if we remind ourselves of our purpose, we'll move with more strength, courage, and confidence.

## Retrain Your Brain

The recognition that our thoughts drive so much of our physiological reactions is key to overcoming anxiety, depression, and panic. And we shouldn't be surprised. Scripture is replete with insights about the power of the mind to shape our perspectives. You'll find many of these Scriptures in the pages ahead to assist you in the renewing of your mind.

If you are alive, your brain has already been trained. The question is, has your brain been trained toward anxiety and fear, or toward confidence and resilience? If it's the former, how do you retrain your brain—your reactions, emotions, habits, life patterns—to produce resilience?

We rewire our brains by taking the time to understand why we are processing information in certain ways and then find new ways to pursue change.

When we begin to ask ourselves what triggers those emotions and behaviors, we'll be able to determine a plan of attack whenever those negative emotions and behaviors rise up. In time, we'll look back and find that our ability to trade negative thinking for a life of mental resilience was a matter of brain training. The payoff for training our brains now will show up when we need it most—even in our darkest hour.

## Know the Truth That Sets Free

Living our lives as if we're slaves to circumstances locks us in mental, emotional, and spiritual bondage. And in spiritual bondage, it's impossible to find resilience. But as Jesus taught, renewing our minds and living in the truth of the Scriptures is the best way to break free. This simply means spending time searching out and understanding all that Jesus says. It means orienting our lives around these truths—whether they come from Jesus' specific words, the wisdom taught in Ecclesiastes and Proverbs, or the teachings of Paul. If we do these things, we will be set free. We can experience the resilience that comes when we fully trust, fully believe, and fully live into God's truth.

# Rule Three | Embrace Adversity:
## *Train with Resistance*

Resilience is a muscle developed through responding to adversity in the right ways. Just as physical exercise increases the body's capacity to handle and offload stress, so too do emotional and spiritual exercise. For this rule, I analogize resilience to a muscle, showing how it can only be built through resistance training. And like any other kind of training, the muscle of resilience must be built through the application of certain training rules.

Rule Three shows us how to build the muscle of resilience as we apply the following training rules: *treat anxiety as a friend, train with resistance, and grow incrementally.*

## What Anxiety Can You Press Into?

We can learn so much from pressing into the pain and asking, "*Why?*" Through pressing in, we come to realize that our fear, pain, and anxiety have something to teach us. These experiences drive us toward God and ask us to meditate on his truths. They show us the areas where we haven't yet surrendered our lives to the reality of his freedom. And it exposes the areas of our lives where we need greater resilience.

No matter what your anxiety is, invite God into it and you'll discover the power that comes when you face your anxiety and surrender it. As you do, you'll experience greater levels of freedom and find that you're building a more resilient life.

## Training with Resistance

Although we can't stop death and decline, we can live resilient, healthy lives while we are here. As it relates to our health, the key question to ask ourselves in building a resilient life is this: *How much resistance training am I willing to do?*

If anxiety is our friend, resistance is our new best friend! You need it. I need it. We can't grow without it. There is only one problem. We've been conditioned our entire lives to avoid the resistance of hard things.

Even the word *resistance* conjures up undesirable feelings, not only in the physical realm, but in the emotional and relational realms as well. None of us want to experience resistance in relationships, whether marriage, business, or friendships. It's normal to seek the path of least resistance. However, in building a life of resilience, and especially when it comes to physical and mental endurance, we must change our orientation. Resistance is not the enemy. Resistance is our ally.

When we train with resistance, we build muscle, gain strength, and accomplish impossible feats. Instead of hitting plateaus and declining, our bodies become more resilient.

### Grow Incrementally

How we invest our time matters. Forming the daily habits and rhythms that keep us in a healthy place is a game plan for rewiring our brains. Making sure our inputs allow us to rest and restore in the healthiest of ways primes our minds and bodies for the outputs of connecting and creating. Building a resilient life requires both the daily habits of incremental growth and the developmental mastery of new skills.

We can change if we commit to slow, intentional, incremental growth. Determine the areas of your life where you need more resilience. Then chart a course for incremental change and see what happens.

## Rule Four | Make Meaning:
### *Cultivate Beauty*

As we embrace adversity, we begin to build the strength necessary to overcome new challenges with a hopeful outlook. When we live this way, we open ourselves to becoming a creative force with God at work in our lives. And by working together with him, we can help create meaning in the world around us. This meaning gives us true purpose, allowing us to solidify our resilience. If we're going to be resilient people, it's imperative that we become people who make meaning.

Rule Four explains how encountering beauty and making good

things can help us cultivate purpose and create meaning. Through these practices, we'll be able to stave off any crisis of meaninglessness and become people of greater resilience.

## Follow the Longing

Longing is the plight of all God's creatures. When we feel a deep ache, a longing for something missing, what we desire most is the presence of God in our everyday moments, maybe particularly in those places where he currently feels absent. And if the resulting silence lingers longer than we're comfortable with, even days into weeks, we tend to fill that silence with noise, consumption, or adrenaline. Instead, follow the longing, and you'll begin to notice what you really want. When I considered this question of what I really wanted, I discovered that our hearts, minds, and souls most desperately want to love and be loved by real people in real time and space. We want to be seen and known in the absence of shame. We want to engage in meaningful work that leaves us grateful—work in which we've left a part of ourselves. And we long for adventure and risk, play, and human creativity that leave us grateful. We were made for beauty and made to serve beauty.

This process of naming my desire for beauty shifted my thinking. It made me slow down and look for beauty in the world around me. It made me less reactive and required me to consider how I wanted to live my life in an intentional and lasting pursuit for the beautiful things that matter in life. Naming your desire will do the same for you.

## Resilient People Encounter Beauty and Restore Beauty

Beauty is the antidote to scarcity. When we live in fear, we see lack. When we recognize beauty, we encounter the divine. But encountering beauty isn't just about noticing natural beauty in the world around you; it's also about noticing the beautiful things God has planted in you and then allowing those things to flourish. It's about reclaiming our creativity and seeing how this creativity is a God-given thing.

If you want to overcome your compulsions and anxious obsessions, begin to look for beauty in the world around you. As you do, you'll find more joy and fulfillment. You'll find a light to guide you through the darkness. You'll find a rest that the world can't fathom.

## Create Flourishing Spaces

We all need spaces that allow us to be restored. In the bustle of everyday life, our souls need order. In my home, I set out to create spaces that invite the kind of soul rest that allows me to go out into the world with more strength and inspiration. Furthermore, we need spaces that challenge us, like the gym or a therapist's office, as well as spaces that inspire and connect us, such as the places we gather for a Bible study.

With a little intention, any space can become a resilience-making space. Whether it's a space to recharge and rejuvenate so we can face the challenges of the world, an intentional place of resistance, or a place of connection, spaces create the conditions in which we can become better versions of ourselves. When we create these kinds of intentional spaces, we become those better versions and help others see that building a resilient life is possible.

## Make Good Things

When we make good things, we partner with God in his epic plan to bless the world. He doesn't need us but he chooses us! He longs to be with us, inspire us, and renew his world through us. He has given us the ability to imagine and create solutions for the world's problems.

The act of making good things doesn't have to be grandiose. It can be as simple as making someone cookies, writing a letter to a friend, or creating a small backyard garden. These little things can fill you with purpose and give meaning to your day-to-day existence.

There is no doubt that God designed your mind, body, and soul to make things. Because you are made in his image, when you create, you are infused with his imagination to set the world right. That's why creating and cultivating does wonders for building your strength of mind and body, the foundations of a resilient life. How could you not be more resilient when you're collaborating with God?

## Rule Five | Endure Together: *Invite Others In*

The final rule—Rule Five—asks us to be resilient people in a resilient community. Building a resilient life can't be done alone. Living resiliently requires intention to come alongside others, embrace diversity, and enjoy the bounty of community.

### Lock Arms, Link Lives

Mankind was not made for isolation. We were made to be in relationship with both God and one another. The entire story of the Bible—from Genesis to Revelation—bears this out. Still, our culture is becoming increasingly isolated. We're living in a season of seemingly unending adversity and social isolation, which has had an effect on our mental health. Yet resilience isn't found in the power of me; resilience is formed in the power of *we*. We are stronger and more resilient when we commit to a common cause with like-minded people. Resilience grows with common commitment.

### Build Small and Strong

To choose a different way of life in this technologically advanced, modernized world isn't only outrageous, but it requires all kinds of resilience.

In a culture obsessed with size, we've been trained to believe that bigger is better. It's a near-inescapable mentality because it's all we've ever known. However, throughout history, the most resilient communities were small and far more focused on how they could take care of their needs with local resources. They were bands, clans, and tribes that shared land, family ancestry, religion, and agricultural interest. They worked together to ensure their collective survival. The resilience of a community is not dependent on the size; its vision is to cultivate communities of people committed to doing what God asks.

## Harness the Power of We

We are a communal people created by a communal God. Jesus recognized that the church is made up of individuals who believe in him, but he did not simply pray for the individuals alone. He prayed for them together, in community. He prayed for our relationships with one another, that we would experience the kind of relationship he has with God the Father, a relationship of complete unity.

In *Building a Resilient Life*, I write how about how, in unified commitment, my local community found a more holistic version of resilience. We didn't rely on ourselves but became an unshakable community that helped meet the needs of one another. This vision began to spread on a broader scale to friends in other cities.

## We Were Made to Need One Another

We live in an individualistic society, one that teaches us that self-sufficiency *is* resilience. But we were not created to resist adversity alone. Research indicates that a strong support system or a community that is resilient during times of adversity allows us to bounce back more easily.

True community reminds you who you really are. A community of like-minded people calls forth the character and integrity they believe you embody. They hold you accountable so that your inside matches your outside, your private life matches your public life. They remind you that you're stronger than you think, braver than you think, more loved than you think. A Christ-centered community encourages you to grow in your connection to Christ as well, which makes you infinitely more resilient.

Christ-centered community encourages us to use our gifts for the good of the group and to press into our purpose and calling.

# RESILIENT PRACTICES

## RULE ONE: NAME THE PAIN

Reflect and journal.

List ways you've grown and are practicing resilience building.

Create a gratitude list.

Confess your anxieties.

Take inventory of your overwhelm.

Spend time in solitude.

Read and pray Psalm 139.

Uncover your shame.

Try seeing a counselor or therapist.

Go on a retreat.

Ask a loved one to help identify shame, wounds, and pain in your life.

Name your feelings.

Identify current adversities.

Observe how your body may be revealing shame or pain.

Examine how you may be triggering shame in others.

Search your heart to see if there is anyone you need to forgive.

## OTHER

..................................................................................

..................................................................................

..................................................................................

..................................................................................

..................................................................................

..................................................................................

..................................................................................

..................................................................................

..................................................................................

..................................................................................

..................................................................................

..................................................................................

..................................................................................

..................................................................................

# RULE TWO: SHIFT THE NARRATIVE

Meditate on Scripture.

Play a brain game.

Read a personal growth book.

Memorize your favorite verse.

Identify toxic thoughts and replace them with the truth of Scripture.

Take inventory of media inputs and evaluate how they influence your thoughts.

Choose a life verse.

Write out three promises from Scripture.

List three books to read that will inspire you.

Add "think" time to your calendar.

Create space and invite God to speak to you.

Reflect on moments in which you've experienced anxious thoughts.

Journal the toxic thoughts that haunt you regularly.

Write out a plan to take thoughts captive when needed.

Pray Scripture out loud.

Listen to a podcast.

## OTHER

........................................................................................................

........................................................................................................

........................................................................................................

........................................................................................................

........................................................................................................

........................................................................................................

........................................................................................................

# RULE THREE: EMBRACE ADVERSITY

Engage with someone you've been avoiding.

Go for a bike ride.

Take a hike in nature.

Tackle a difficult task at home.

Take a strength-building class at the gym.

Take an online master class in an area of interest.

Stretch your body in the morning or in the evening before bed.

Read a personal growth book.

Walk ten thousand steps today.

Dance in your kitchen and get your heart rate up.

Journal about an area you'd like to grow in during this week.

Start a Bible reading plan.

Make healthy food choices.

Confront toxic thoughts with Scripture.

Plan four days this week for a brisk forty-five-minute walk.

Try taking a new class at a gym.

## OTHER

..............................................    ..............................................
..............................................    ..............................................
..............................................    ..............................................
..............................................    ..............................................
..............................................    ..............................................
..............................................    ..............................................
..............................................    ..............................................

# RULE FOUR: MAKE MEANING

Start an herb garden.

Learn to make bread.

Write a poem or song.

Try out a new recipe.

Make a candle.

Learn to knit, sew, or crochet.

Plant a garden.

Take an art class.

Declutter your home.

Bake something and share it with a neighbor.

Repair something that needs mending.

Watercolor the view from your front door.

Volunteer for a good cause.

Reflect on where your talents and burdens intersect.

Make a space in your home beautiful.

Grow flowers from seeds.

## OTHER

....................................................................    ....................................................................

....................................................................    ....................................................................

....................................................................    ....................................................................

....................................................................    ....................................................................

....................................................................    ....................................................................

....................................................................    ....................................................................

....................................................................    ....................................................................

# RULE FIVE: ENDURE TOGETHER

Take a walk with a friend.

Play a game.

Call a long-distance friend.

Invite a family over for a meal.

Volunteer at your church or for an organization.

Send a card or letter of encouragement.

Pray together with your family.

Start or join a community Bible study.

Initiate a vulnerable conversation.

Pray with someone in need.

Apologize when necessary and seek forgiveness.

Forgive others who have hurt you.

Invite a neighbor over for coffee.

Text a Scripture to a friend in need.

Plan a video call that will reunite old friends.

Meet a tangible need (e.g., babysit, help clean someone's home, cook a meal).

Share a prayer request you have.

## OTHER

......................................................................................................

......................................................................................................

......................................................................................................

......................................................................................................

......................................................................................................

......................................................................................................

......................................................................................................

Welcome to your first month and first rule. In these next four weeks, as you embark on a journey to build resilience, your focus will be to name your pain and to be honest with yourself, as well as with others. You'll examine your life and begin to identify areas of pain that you may not have been able to name up to this point. Having this insight into your life is a necessary place to start, but we won't stop there. You weren't created to carry your struggles alone. To grow in strength, hope, and meaning, it's essential to connect with others and let others in—to both confess your pain and receive empathy. Don't worry, each time you practice vulnerability, you'll find that it becomes easier. And you can reciprocate and offer a listening ear and show empathy to a friend or family member in need. Examining your heart, identifying struggles, acknowledging the need for confession, and practicing forgiveness are the building blocks of a resilient life.

## MONTH ONE
## RULE ONE

---

# NAME
# THE PAIN

---

## BE HONEST

# MONTHLY CALENDAR

**MONTH**

| MONDAY | TUESDAY | WEDNESDAY | THURSDAY |
|--------|---------|-----------|----------|
|        |         |           |          |
|        |         |           |          |
|        |         |           |          |
|        |         |           |          |
|        |         |           |          |

*The antidote to shame is the vulnerability to expose it.*

—REBEKAH LYONS

| FRIDAY | SATURDAY | SUNDAY |
|---|---|---|
|  |  |  |
|  |  |  |
|  |  |  |
|  |  |  |
|  |  |  |

**TOP PRIORITIES**

. . . . . . .
. . . . . . .
. . . . . . .
. . . . . . .
. . . . . . .

**RESILIENCE GOALS**

. . . . . . .
. . . . . . .
. . . . . . .
. . . . . . .
. . . . . . .

# RULE ONE / SCRIPTURES

Take time to meditate on the following Scriptures this month. They are here for you to return to as you Name the Pain.

The LORD himself goes before you and will be with you; he will never leave you nor forsake you. Do not be afraid; do not be discouraged.

—DEUTERONOMY 31:8

"Go and make disciples . . . teaching them to obey everything I have commanded you. And surely I am with you always, to the very end of the age."

—MATTHEW 28:19–20

Those who are led by the Spirit of God are the children of God. The Spirit you received does not make you slaves, so that you live in fear again; rather, the Spirit you received brought about your adoption to sonship. And by him we cry, "*Abba*, Father." The Spirit himself testifies with our spirit that we are God's children. Now if we are children, then we are heirs—heirs of God and co-heirs with Christ, if indeed we share in his sufferings in order that we may also share in his glory.

—ROMANS 8:14–17

"I won't lay anything heavy or ill-fitting on you. Keep company with me and you'll learn to live freely and lightly."

—MATTHEW 11:28 MSG

I heard a loud voice from the throne saying, "Look! God's dwelling place is now among the people, and he will dwell with them. They

will be his people, and God himself will be with them and be their
God."

—REVELATION 21:3

"In this world you will have trouble. But take heart! I have
overcome the world."

—JOHN 16:33

Consider it pure joy, my brothers and sisters, whenever you face
trials of many kinds, because you know that the testing of your faith
produces perseverance. Let perseverance finish its work so that you
may be mature and complete, not lacking anything.

—JAMES 1:2–4

Praise be to the God and Father of our Lord Jesus Christ . . . who
comforts us in all our troubles, so that we can comfort those in any
trouble with the comfort we ourselves receive from God.

—2 CORINTHIANS 1:3–4

We do not have a high priest who is unable to empathize with
our weaknesses, but we have one who has been tempted in every
way, just as we are—yet he did not sin. Let us then approach God's
throne of grace with confidence, so that we may receive mercy and
find grace to help us in our time of need.

—HEBREWS 4:15–16

COMFORT

Therefore we do not despair, but even if our physical body is wearing away, our inner person is being renewed day by day.

—2 CORINTHIANS 4:16 NET

I don't say this out of need, for I have learned to be content in whatever circumstances I find myself. I know how to make do with little, and I know how to make do with a lot. In any and all circumstances I have learned the secret of being content—whether well fed or hungry, whether in abundance or in need. I am able to do all things through [Christ] who strengthens me.

—PHILIPPIANS 4:11–13 CSB

Therefore we do not lose heart. Though outwardly we are wasting away, yet inwardly we are being renewed day by day. For our light and momentary troubles are achieving for us an eternal glory that far outweighs them all. So we fix our eyes not on what is seen, but on what is unseen, since what is seen is temporary, but what is unseen is eternal.

—2 CORINTHIANS 4:16–18

If we confess our sins, [God] is faithful and just and will forgive us our sins and purify us from all unrighteousness.

—1 JOHN 1:9

During the days of Jesus' life on earth, he offered up prayers and petitions with fervent cries and tears to the one who could save him from death, and he was heard because of his reverent submission. Son though he was, he learned obedience from what he suffered and, once made perfect, he became the source of eternal salvation for all who obey him.

—HEBREWS 5:7–9

Search me, God, and know my heart;
    test me and know my anxious thoughts.
See if there is any offensive way in me,
    and lead me in the way everlasting.

—PSALM 139:23–24

EXAMINE

Whoever eats the bread or drinks the cup of the Lord in an unworthy manner will be guilty of sinning against the body and blood of the Lord. Everyone ought to examine themselves before they eat of the bread and drink from the cup. For those who eat and drink without discerning the body of Christ eat and drink judgment on themselves. That is why many among you are weak and sick, and a number of you have fallen asleep.

—1 CORINTHIANS 11:27–30

If you forgive other people when they sin against you, your heavenly Father will also forgive you.

—MATTHEW 6:14

# WEEKLY PRACTICE

*"I won't lay anything heavy or ill-fitting on you. Keep company with me and you'll learn to live freely and lightly."*
—MATTHEW 11:28 MSG

## GOAL
This week I intend (purpose) to:

## INTENTION
I will take action by:

## FOCUS
My Scripture to meditate on is:

## GRATITUDE
This week I'm grateful for:

## PRACTICES
◎ Reflect and journal.
◎ List ways you are practicing resilience.
◎ List ways you've grown.
◎ .............................................................................................................
◎ .............................................................................................................

# *EXAMINE*

What areas of shame have you experienced in the past?
In more recent times? Describe the situation(s).

Can you identify what your shame response looks like? When faced with rejection, what is your typical reaction? Do you have a physical response? Are you detecting any patterns? Describe them.

Shame can be difficult to uncover, but once you do, it's important to bring it into the light. Have you shared areas of shame in your life with a trusted person? If not, take a moment to think about someone in your life who might be a safe and trusted person you can be vulnerable with.

# *REVIEW*

## HOW DID YOU DO THIS WEEK?

I'M FEELING:

MY FAVORITE ACTIVITY:

ONE THING I LEARNED
ABOUT MYSELF:

I GREW IN STRENGTH BY:

I GREW IN HOPE BY:

I GREW IN MEANING BY:

WEEKLY WINS:

ONE THING I IDENTIFIED ABOUT SHAME:

THE MOST IMPORTANT THING I DISCOVERED ABOUT
RULE ONE THIS PAST WEEK:

I'D LIKE TO GROW IN THE FOLLOWING WAY:

NEXT WEEK I WANT TO FOCUS ON:

# WEEKLY PRACTICE

*Be slow to fall into friendship; but when thou art in, continue firm and constant.*
—SOCRATES

## GOAL
This week I intend (purpose) to:

## INTENTION
I will take action by:

## FOCUS
My Scripture to meditate on is:

## GRATITUDE
This week I'm grateful for:

## PRACTICES
- ○ Take inventory of your overwhelm.
- ○ Spend time in solitude.
- ○ Pray Psalm 139.
- ○ .............................................................................................
- ○ .............................................................................................

# EXAMINE

If you were to feel free to be transparent and vulnerable with a friend, what one thing would you want to bring into the light and share? What have you been trying to carry on your own?

In what ways have you been practicing being open and honest with others? Do you find it easy or difficult? How will you practice getting honest and letting others in during this week?

When you invited others in and got honest, how did you feel after you shared? What surprised you about the experience of sharing your pain?

# *REVIEW*

## HOW DID YOU DO THIS WEEK?

I'M FEELING:

MY FAVORITE ACTIVITY:

ONE THING I LEARNED
ABOUT MYSELF:

I GREW IN STRENGTH BY:

I GREW IN HOPE BY:

I GREW IN MEANING BY:

WEEKLY WINS:

I INVITED THE FOLLOWING PEOPLE IN:

THE MOST IMPORTANT THING I DISCOVERED ABOUT
RULE ONE THIS PAST WEEK:

I'D LIKE TO GROW IN THE FOLLOWING WAY:

NEXT WEEK I WANT TO FOCUS ON:

# WEEKLY PRACTICE

*The rhythm of confession becomes a rhythm of healing.*
—REBEKAH LYONS

## GOAL
This week I intend (purpose) to:

## INTENTION
I will take action by:

## FOCUS
My Scripture to meditate on is:

## GRATITUDE
This week I'm grateful for:

## PRACTICES
○ Try seeing a counselor or therapist.
○ Go on a one-day retreat.
○ Journal your feelings.
○ ....................................................................................
○ ....................................................................................

# EXAMINE

For healing to be possible, God gave us the practice of confession, both to him and to one another. When you hear the word *confession*, what comes to mind? In what ways have you participated in confession in the past? How will you engage in confession this week?

In *Building a Resilient Life*, Rebekah talks about the "highly edited version" of ourselves, which is the self we put out there for people to see. What does your highly edited version look like? What do you edit for others? Do you edit or withhold anything from God?

The practice of confession cultivates renewed resilience. Now that you're putting intention into a practice of confession, describe a time when you confessed and shared a weakness with others. What was their response? How did you feel after sharing?

# REVIEW

## HOW DID YOU DO THIS WEEK?

I'M FEELING:

MY FAVORITE ACTIVITY:

ONE THING I LEARNED
ABOUT MYSELF:

I GREW IN STRENGTH BY:

I GREW IN HOPE BY:

I GREW IN MEANING BY:

WEEKLY WINS:

I GAVE AND/OR RECEIVED EMPATHY BY:

THE MOST IMPORTANT THING I DISCOVERED ABOUT
RULE ONE THIS PAST WEEK:

I'D LIKE TO GROW IN THE FOLLOWING WAY:

NEXT WEEK I WANT TO FOCUS ON:

# WEEKLY PRACTICE

*We confess our brokenness to God and one another so that we may be healed.*
—REBEKAH LYONS

## GOAL
This week I intend (purpose) to:

## INTENTION
I will take action by:

## FOCUS
My Scripture to meditate on is:

## GRATITUDE
This week I'm grateful for:

## PRACTICES
○ Identify current adversities.
○ Observe how your body may be revealing shame or pain.
○ Search your heart to see if there is anyone you need to forgive.
○ ....................................................................................
○ ....................................................................................

# *EXAMINE*

How can you "go first" this week in letting others in and confessing? Are you willing to create an environment in which others can find freedom to share and confess? Who might you do this with?

What does the practice of forgiveness look like in your life? Are you holding on to any hurt, bitterness, or contempt? Is there anyone specific whom you need to forgive?

Pray the words of Psalm 139:23–24: "Search me, God, and know my heart; test me and know my anxious thoughts. See if there is any offensive way in me, and lead me in the way everlasting." Ask the Lord to reveal anything that you have kept hidden. What did you hear? Conclude by writing a personal prayer of confession to God.

# REVIEW

## HOW DID YOU DO THIS WEEK?

I'M FEELING:

MY FAVORITE ACTIVITY:

ONE THING I LEARNED
ABOUT MYSELF:

I GREW IN STRENGTH BY:

I GREW IN HOPE BY:

I GREW IN MEANING BY:

WEEKLY WINS:

I ENGAGED IN THE RHYTHM OF CONFESSION BY:

THE MOST IMPORTANT THING I DISCOVERED ABOUT
RULE ONE THIS PAST WEEK:

I'D LIKE TO GROW IN THE FOLLOWING WAY:

NEXT WEEK I WANT TO FOCUS ON:

# MONTHLY REVIEW

## HOW WELL DID YOU DO THIS MONTH?

Take time to check in with yourself to review your growth and progress. Notice how you've grown, and reflect on how you'd like to make further progress next month.

What about "naming the pain" came naturally for you? Why?

What about "naming the pain" did you find most difficult? Why?

Which goals or priorities were you able to meet? Are there any you would like to continue to work toward?

## Rule One

The thing that surprised me most about myself was:

I want to improve next month by:

On a scale of 1 to 10, circle how resilient you're feeling this month.

1    2    3    4    5    6    7    8    9    10

## NOTES

Let's keep building. This next month, you'll give time and attention to shifting the narrative in your life and renewing your mind. Whether we realize it or not, we all have narratives, or stories, that we tell ourselves about our own lives and the world around us. These narratives are powerful because they influence how we perceive and respond to people and situations around us. This month offers opportunities to face negative thought patterns head-on, to retrain and rewire your brain, and to use Scripture to reveal truth and preach to yourself. As you start to face toxic thoughts and anxieties, you'll cultivate resilience in the realm of mental health.

# MONTH TWO
## RULE TWO

---

# SHIFT THE
# NARRATIVE

---

## RENEW YOUR
## MIND

# MONTHLY CALENDAR

MONTH

| MONDAY | TUESDAY | WEDNESDAY | THURSDAY |
|--------|---------|-----------|----------|
|        |         |           |          |
|        |         |           |          |
|        |         |           |          |
|        |         |           |          |
|        |         |           |          |

*Blessed is the one . . . whose delight is in the law of the LORD,
and who meditates on his law day and night.
That person is like a tree planted by streams of water,
which yields its fruit in season
and whose leaf does not wither.*

—PSALM 1:1–3

| FRIDAY | SATURDAY | SUNDAY |
|---|---|---|
| | | |
| | | |
| | | |
| | | |
| | | |

**TOP PRIORITIES**

RESILIENCE GOALS

# RULE TWO / SCRIPTURES

Take time to meditate on the following Scriptures this month.
They are here for you to return to as you Shift the Narrative.

Blessed is the one . . . whose delight is in the law of
> the LORD,
> and who meditates on his law day and night.
That person is like a tree planted by streams of water,
> which yields its fruit in season
and whose leaf does not wither.

—PSALM 1:1–3

Finally, brothers and sisters, whatever is true, whatever is noble,
whatever is right, whatever is pure, whatever is lovely, whatever is
admirable—if anything is excellent or praiseworthy—think about
such things.

—PHILIPPIANS 4:8

I meditate on your precepts
> and consider your ways.

—PSALM 119:15

I will ponder all your work,
> and meditate on your mighty deeds.

—PSALM 77:12 ESV

I have stored up your word in my heart,
> that I might not sin against you.

—PSALM 119:11 ESV

Without faith it is impossible to please God, because anyone who comes to him must believe that he exists and that he rewards those who earnestly seek him.

—HEBREWS 11:6

Therefore, I urge you, brothers and sisters, in view of God's mercy, to offer your bodies as a living sacrifice, holy and pleasing to God—this is your true and proper worship. Do not conform to the pattern of this world, but be transformed by the renewing of your mind. Then you will be able to test and approve what God's will is—his good, pleasing and perfect will.

—ROMANS 12:1–2

FAITH

Be alert and of sober mind. Your enemy the devil prowls around like a roaring lion looking for someone to devour.

—1 PETER 5:8

With minds that are alert and fully sober, set your hope on the grace to be brought to you when Jesus Christ is revealed at his coming.

—1 PETER 1:13

Therefore we do not lose heart. Though outwardly we are wasting away, yet inwardly we are being renewed day by day.

—2 CORINTHIANS 4:16

Faith comes from hearing, and hearing through the word of Christ.

—ROMANS 10:17 ESV

The word of God is alive and active. Sharper than any double-edged sword, it penetrates even to dividing soul and spirit, joints and marrow; it judges the thoughts and attitudes of the heart.

—HEBREWS 4:12

Seek first the kingdom of God and his righteousness, and all these things will be added to you.

—MATTHEW 6:33 ESV

[Jesus] answered, "It is written,
'Man shall not live by bread alone,
    but by every word that comes from the mouth of
        God.'"

—MATTHEW 4:4 ESV

"You will know the truth, and the truth will set you free."

—JOHN 8:32

All Scripture is breathed out by God and profitable for teaching, for reproof, for correction, and for training in righteousness, that the man of God may be complete, equipped for every good work.

—2 TIMOTHY 3:16–17 ESV

Set your minds on things that are above, not on things that are on earth.

—COLOSSIANS 3:2 ESV

You keep him in perfect peace
    whose mind is stayed on you,
    because he trusts in you.

—ISAIAH 26:3 ESV

"Peace I leave with you; my peace I give you. I do not give to you as the world gives. Do not let your hearts be troubled and do not be afraid."

—JOHN 14:27

Even though I walk
　　through the darkest valley,
I will fear no evil,
　　for you are with me;
your rod and your staff,
　　they comfort me.

—PSALM 23:4

"Do not let your hearts be troubled. You believe in God; believe also in me."

—JOHN 14:1

# WEEKLY PRACTICE

*You get to decide what you say to yourself.*
—SADIE ROBERTSON

## GOAL
This week I intend (purpose) to:

## INTENTION
I will take action by:

## FOCUS
My Scripture to meditate on is:

## GRATITUDE
This week I'm grateful for:

## PRACTICES
○ Meditate on Scripture.
○ Play a brain game.
○ Read a personal growth book.
○ ............................................................................................................
○ ............................................................................................................

# EXAMINE

Narratives help us make sense of the stories we tell ourselves. What narratives, or stories, do you tell yourself? Take a moment to be honest about what plays on repeat in your mind. Pay particular attention to the stories that do not align with God's truth.

Thinking back to the narratives you uncovered, begin creating a new narrative to replace the old. What truths in Scripture cancel the lie or lies that you've been telling yourself? What truth do you need to tell yourself? How will you meditate on God's Word to renew your mind this coming week?

Renewing the mind requires getting serious about the thoughts we have, books we read, content we let in, and ideas we've come to trust. We must become vigilant about how we think, what we think, and what inputs we allow in. Think through your inputs and do an audit. Are there any books, shows, social media accounts, news media, or websites that are having a negative impact on your heart and soul? How do you think your input affects your attitude, fears, and longings? Is there anything you need to omit?

# REVIEW

## HOW DID YOU DO THIS WEEK?

I'M FEELING:

MY FAVORITE ACTIVITY:

ONE THING I LEARNED
ABOUT MYSELF:

I GREW IN STRENGTH BY:

I GREW IN HOPE BY:

I GREW IN MEANING BY:

WEEKLY WINS:

A NARRATIVE I'M SHIFTING:

THE MOST IMPORTANT THING I DISCOVERED ABOUT
RULE TWO THIS PAST WEEK:

I'D LIKE TO GROW IN THE FOLLOWING WAY:

NEXT WEEK I WANT TO FOCUS ON:

# WEEKLY PRACTICE

*Today is going to be a great day!*
—DR. DANIEL AMEN

## GOAL
This week I intend (purpose) to:

## INTENTION
I will take action by:

## FOCUS
My Scripture to meditate on is:

## GRATITUDE
This week I'm grateful for:

## PRACTICES
- ◯ Identify toxic thoughts and replace them with the truth of Scripture.
- ◯ Take inventory of media inputs and evaluate their influence on your thoughts.
- ◯ Write out three promises from Scripture.
- ◯ ........................................................
- ◯ ........................................................

# *EXAMINE*

How do you start your day? Be honest with yourself. Do you approach your day feeling overwhelmed and exhausted? When negative thoughts come to mind throughout the day, do you agree with them? How is this serving you?

Now that you've seen areas where your brain is on autopilot, how can you begin to take charge of those thoughts and feelings that have been driving your attitude, your energy, and the way your day plays out?

Let's go a little deeper and pinpoint where your mind directs its attention. Do you struggle with negative thoughts? Are you tempted to focus on your brokenness, failure, and weakness? Do you dwell on your anxieties? Or is it something else? Write about this.

RULE TWO | WEEK TWO

# *REVIEW*

## HOW DID YOU DO THIS WEEK?

I'M FEELING:

MY FAVORITE ACTIVITY:

ONE THING I LEARNED ABOUT MYSELF:

I GREW IN STRENGTH BY:

I GREW IN HOPE BY:

I GREW IN MEANING BY:

WEEKLY WINS:

ONE WAY I RENEWED MY MIND:

THE MOST IMPORTANT THING I DISCOVERED ABOUT
RULE TWO THIS PAST WEEK:

I'D LIKE TO GROW IN THE FOLLOWING WAY:

NEXT WEEK I WANT TO FOCUS ON:

# WEEKLY PRACTICE

*We don't become what we dream; we become what we think.*
—REBEKAH LYONS

## GOAL
This week I intend (purpose) to:

## INTENTION
I will take action by:

## FOCUS
My Scripture to meditate on is:

## GRATITUDE
This week I'm grateful for:

## PRACTICES
○ List three books to read that will inspire you.
○ Add "think" time to your calendar.
○ Create space and invite God to speak to you.
○ ......................................................................................
○ ......................................................................................

RULE TWO | WEEK THREE

# EXAMINE

How we think about our circumstances and where we choose to put our focus directly impacts how we experience life. Last week, you uncovered the focus of your thoughts. This week, spend a few minutes creating a new focus. Write out Scriptures and statements of truth you will use to preach to yourself this week.

We rewire our brains by taking the time to understand why we process information certain ways and resolve to pursue change. What triggers you to respond in fear, anxiety, depression, addiction, and the like? Name any places, people, activities, or situations that trigger you. Can you pinpoint an origin or root cause?

Now that you've identified your triggers, get creative and begin to strategize and then build a routine to respond when you face a difficult situation. Ask the Holy Spirit for wisdom as you seek to determine three simple steps to put into practice. Commit to working on that this week.

# *REVIEW*

## HOW DID YOU DO THIS WEEK?

I'M FEELING:

MY FAVORITE ACTIVITY:

ONE THING I LEARNED
ABOUT MYSELF:

I GREW IN STRENGTH BY:

I GREW IN HOPE BY:

I GREW IN MEANING BY:

WEEKLY WINS:

A ROUTINE OR HABIT I'M FINDING HELPFUL TO RETRAIN MY
BRAIN:

THE MOST IMPORTANT THING I DISCOVERED ABOUT
RULE TWO THIS PAST WEEK:

I'D LIKE TO GROW IN THE FOLLOWING WAY:

NEXT WEEK I WANT TO FOCUS ON:

# WEEKLY PRACTICE

*If you hold to my teaching, you are really my disciples. Then you will know the truth, and the truth will set you free.*
—JOHN 8:31B–32

## GOAL
This week I intend (purpose) to:

## INTENTION
I will take action by:

## FOCUS
My Scripture to meditate on is:

## GRATITUDE
This week I'm grateful for:

## PRACTICES
- ○ Journal the toxic thoughts that haunt you regularly.
- ○ Write out a plan to take thoughts captive when needed.
- ○ Pray Scripture out loud.
- ○ .................................................................................................
- ○ .................................................................................................

# EXAMINE

Living your life as if you're a slave to circumstances locks you in mental, emotional, and spiritual bondage. And in spiritual bondage, it's impossible to find resilience. Have you ever felt like a slave to your circumstances or in bondage mentally, emotionally, or spiritually? Describe the circumstance and be honest about why you felt that way.

What is your relationship with Scripture? Do you believe it to be truth? The prophet Ezekiel describes consuming the words of Scripture as tasting as sweet as honey (see Ezekiel 3:3). And the writer of the book of Hebrews says, "The word of God is alive and active. Sharper than any double-edged sword, it penetrates even to dividing soul and spirit, joints and marrow; it judges the thoughts and attitudes of the heart" (Hebrews 4:12). We learn the truth by reading, studying, and understanding God's Word, which speaks to all of life. Are you open to spending time in God's Word?

Think of someone you know who has lived a life of pursuing truth, even in the midst of difficult circumstances. What characteristics did that person embody? What strength do or did you see in them? Write about their influence and what you admire most about them. If they're still living, consider sharing with them what you wrote.

# REVIEW

## HOW DID YOU DO THIS WEEK?

I'M FEELING:

MY FAVORITE ACTIVITY:

ONE THING I LEARNED
ABOUT MYSELF:

I GREW IN STRENGTH BY:

I GREW IN HOPE BY:

I GREW IN MEANING BY:

WEEKLY WINS:

A TRUTH I'M ORIENTATING MY MIND ON:

THE MOST IMPORTANT THING I DISCOVERED ABOUT
RULE TWO THIS PAST WEEK:

I'D LIKE TO GROW IN THE FOLLOWING WAY:

NEXT WEEK I WANT TO FOCUS ON:

# MONTHLY REVIEW

## HOW WELL DID YOU DO THIS MONTH?

Take time to check in with yourself to review your growth and progress. Notice how you've grown, and reflect on how you'd like to make further progress next month.

What about "shifting the narrative" came naturally for you? Why?

What about "shifting the narrative" did you find most difficult? Why?

Which goals or priorities were you able to meet? Are there any you'd like to continue to work toward?

## Rule Two

The thing that surprised me most about myself was:

I want to improve next month by:

On a scale of 1 to 10, circle how resilient you're feeling this month.

1     2     3     4     5     6     7     8     9     10

## NOTES

You are growing stronger each day! In the upcoming month, as you begin to embrace adversity and train with resistance, you'll discover strength you didn't even realize you had. We've focused on building resilience in our hearts and minds and now it's time to engage in training our bodies as well. You'll consider how your body responds to anxiety, how it can teach you what you need to know, how you might be able to push into your pain, and what your current comfort and physical state reveal about where and how you need to train and grow incrementally. That's right, you can grow incrementally by pushing yourself a little further each week and each month. Resilience is a muscle developed through responding to adversity in the right ways. Let's train our bodies and spirits and practice resilience.

## MONTH THREE
## RULE THREE

---

# EMBRACE
# ADVERSITY

---

## TRAIN WITH
## RESISTANCE

# MONTHLY CALENDAR

MONTH

| MONDAY | TUESDAY | WEDNESDAY | THURSDAY |
|--------|---------|-----------|----------|
|        |         |           |          |
|        |         |           |          |
|        |         |           |          |
|        |         |           |          |
|        |         |           |          |

*When we train with resistance, we build muscle, gain strength, and accomplish seemingly impossible feats. Instead of hitting plateaus and declining, we become more resilient.*

—REBEKAH LYONS

| FRIDAY | SATURDAY | SUNDAY |
|---|---|---|
| | | |
| | | |
| | | |
| | | |
| | | |

**TOP PRIORITIES**

**RESILIENCE GOALS**

# RULE THREE | SCRIPTURES

Take time to meditate on the following Scriptures this month. They are here for you to return to as you Embrace Adversity.

Keep this Book of the Law always on your lips; meditate on it day and night, so that you may be careful to do everything written in it. Then you will be prosperous and successful.
—JOSHUA 1:8

My eyes stay open through the watches of the night,
    that I may meditate on your promises.
—PSALM 119:148

May these words of my mouth and this meditation of my
        heart
    be pleasing in your sight,
    Lord, my Rock and my Redeemer.
—PSALM 19:14

My mouth will speak words of wisdom;
    the meditation of my heart will give you understanding.
—PSALM 49:3

I remember the days of long ago;
    I meditate on all your works
    and consider what your hands have done.
—PSALM 143:5

Now go; I will help you speak and will teach you what to say.
—EXODUS 4:12

"The spirit is willing, but the flesh is weak."

—MATTHEW 26:41

We know that in all things God works for the good of those who love him, who have been called according to his purpose.

—ROMANS 8:28

"My grace is sufficient for you, for my power is made perfect in weakness."

—2 CORINTHIANS 12:9

Cast all your anxiety on him because he cares for you.

—1 PETER 5:7

Do you not know that in a race all the runners run, but only one gets the prize? Run in such a way as to get the prize. Everyone who competes in the games goes into strict training. They do it to get a crown that will not last, but we do it to get a crown that will last forever. Therefore I do not run like someone running aimlessly; I do not fight like a boxer beating the air. No, I strike a blow to my body and make it my slave so that after I have preached to others, I myself will not be disqualified for the prize.

—1 CORINTHIANS 9:24-27

"As for you, be strong and do not give up, for your work will be rewarded."

—2 CHRONICLES 15:7

In all these things we are more than conquerors through [Christ] who loved us.

—ROMANS 8:37

I have fought the good fight, I have finished the race, I have kept the faith.

—2 TIMOTHY 4:7

STRENGTH

Blessed are those whose strength is in you,
   whose hearts are set on pilgrimage.

—PSALM 84:5

The LORD gives strength to his people;
   the LORD blesses his people with peace.

—PSALM 29:11

I am the LORD your God,
   who brought you up out of Egypt.
Open wide your mouth and I will fill it.

—PSALM 81:10

We are hard pressed on every side, but not crushed; perplexed, but not in despair; persecuted, but not abandoned; struck down, but not destroyed.

—2 CORINTHIANS 4:8-9

RESCUE

The righteous person may have many troubles,
   but the LORD delivers him from them all.

—PSALM 34:19

If we are children, then we are heirs—heirs of God and co-heirs with Christ, if indeed we share in his sufferings in order that we may also share in his glory. I consider that our present sufferings are not worth comparing with the glory that will be revealed in us.

—ROMANS 8:17-18

As for me, I am poor and needy;
    may the LORD think of me.
You are my help and my deliverer;
    you are my God, do not delay.
—PSALM 40:17

From the LORD comes deliverance.
    May your blessing be on your people.
—PSALM 3:8

# *WEEKLY PRACTICE*

*Resilience is a muscle developed through responding to adversity in the right ways.*
—REBEKAH LYONS

## GOAL
This week I intend (purpose) to:

## INTENTION
I will take action by:

## FOCUS
My Scripture to meditate on is:

## GRATITUDE
This week I'm grateful for:

## PRACTICES
○ Reach out to someone you've missed.
○ Organize a space at home.
○ Take a hike in nature.
○ ...........................................................................
○ ...........................................................................

# EXAMINE

In *Building a Resilient Life*, Rebekah poses a question: "What if adversity is a gift?" What comes to mind when you hear the word *adversity* or ponder the adversity you've faced? Can you view or accept adversity as a gift? Why or why not?

When we turn toward pain and discomfort, we experience less of both. When we focus our thinking—a form of meditation—we display decreased activity in the area of the brain involved in registering pain, as well as increased activity in three areas involved in the regulation of pain. Write about any pain you've been facing and any pain you've been avoiding. Why do you think you might be avoiding the pain?

When you find yourself overcome with fear, anxiety, or panic, what is your typical response? How does your body react? What thoughts play on repeat in your mind? Take a few moments to objectively consider your reactions, responses, and any repetitive patterns.

# REVIEW

## HOW DID YOU DO THIS WEEK?

I'M FEELING:

MY FAVORITE ACTIVITY:

ONE THING I LEARNED
ABOUT MYSELF:

I GREW IN STRENGTH BY:

I GREW IN HOPE BY:

I GREW IN MEANING BY:

WEEKLY WINS:

ONE WAY I'M PRESSING INTO MY PAIN:

THE MOST IMPORTANT THING I DISCOVERED ABOUT
RULE THREE THIS PAST WEEK:

I'D LIKE TO GROW IN THE FOLLOWING WAY:

NEXT WEEK I WANT TO FOCUS ON:

# WEEKLY PRACTICE

*Keep this Book of the Law always on your lips; meditate on it day and night, so that you may be careful to do everything written in it. Then you will be prosperous and successful.*
—JOSHUA 1:8

## GOAL
This week I intend (purpose) to:

## INTENTION
I will take action by:

## FOCUS
My Scripture to meditate on is:

## GRATITUDE
This week I'm grateful for:

## PRACTICES
◯ Walk ten thousand steps today.
◯ Dance in your kitchen and get your heart rate up.
◯ Tackle an outside project (weed the garden, trim the bushes).
◯ ......................................................................................
◯ ......................................................................................

RULE THREE | WEEK TWO

# EXAMINE

Are there any areas of fear or anxiety that are causing you to not live your life fully? In *Building a Resilient Life*, Rebekah shares about a fear of elevators and airplanes. Rather than avoiding it, she chose, with God's help, to expose herself to the anxiety. Are there any areas in your life in which you'd like to consider pressing into the pain, to gently expose yourself to a source of anxiety?

Anxiety can be our friend, meaning it can serve as a barometer that nudges and reveals when all is not well. Sometimes we need to examine our choices, actions, and motivations, and consider where change may be needed. Is there anything in your life that could be adding undue stress and anxiety?

Fear, pain, and anxiety can teach us many things. They can drive us toward God and prompt us to meditate on his truths. Meditating on God's truths can help move us through moments of fear, pain, and anxiety. Find a Scripture that speaks to you and write it out. What is the promise? How will you make an effort to meditate on truth this week?

# REVIEW

## HOW DID YOU DO THIS WEEK?

I'M FEELING:

MY FAVORITE ACTIVITY:

ONE THING I LEARNED
ABOUT MYSELF:

I GREW IN STRENGTH BY:

I GREW IN HOPE BY:

I GREW IN MEANING BY:

WEEKLY WINS:

FOR RESISTANCE TRAINING I DID THE FOLLOWING:

THE MOST IMPORTANT THING I DISCOVERED ABOUT
RULE THREE THIS PAST WEEK:

I'D LIKE TO GROW IN THE FOLLOWING WAY:

NEXT WEEK I WANT TO FOCUS ON:

# WEEKLY PRACTICE

*Resistance is not the enemy; resistance is our ally.*
—REBEKAH LYONS

## GOAL
This week I intend (purpose) to:

## INTENTION
I will take action by:

## FOCUS
My Scripture to meditate on is:

## GRATITUDE
This week I'm grateful for:

## PRACTICES
○ Say no to sugar for the week.
○ Make healthy food choices three days in a row.
○ Exercise in a way that makes you happy.
○ .............................................................................................
○ .............................................................................................

RULE THREE | WEEK THREE
# *EXAMINE*

We don't grow without resistance, and yet we are conditioned to avoid hard things. What hard things have you been avoiding? Why?

When we hear the words "train with resistance," we usually think of physical strength training. Take a moment to consider your current physical health. How do you feel in your body? Strong, weak, energetic, tired? Is there anything your body may be trying to tell you? How would you like to become stronger physically?

Where do you need to build resilience most? Emotionally, spiritually, physically? How can you begin to train with resistance, starting this week?

# *REVIEW*

## HOW DID YOU DO THIS WEEK?

I'M FEELING:

MY FAVORITE ACTIVITY:

ONE THING I LEARNED
ABOUT MYSELF:

I GREW IN STRENGTH BY:

I GREW IN HOPE BY:

I GREW IN MEANING BY:

WEEKLY WINS:

I'M GROWING STRONGER IN MY BODY BY:

THE MOST IMPORTANT THING I DISCOVERED ABOUT
RULE THREE THIS PAST WEEK:

I'D LIKE TO GROW IN THE FOLLOWING WAY:

NEXT WEEK I WANT TO FOCUS ON:

# *WEEKLY PRACTICE*

*You can do almost anything if you are willing to clarify your commitments and make incremental investments over time to achieve them.*
—MICHAEL HYATT

## GOAL
This week I intend (purpose) to:

## INTENTION
I will take action by:

## FOCUS
My Scripture to meditate on is:

## GRATITUDE
This week I'm grateful for:

## PRACTICES
- ○ Do chair dips to strengthen your triceps.
- ○ Plan four days this week for a brisk forty-five-minute walk.
- ○ Do ten pushups.
- ○ ...........................................................................
- ○ ...........................................................................

RULE THREE | WEEK FOUR

# *EXAMINE*

Our earliest experiences affect our brains in profound ways.
Write about an early experience or trauma that continues
to affect you to this day. How would you like to experience
healing and grow emotionally?

Neurogenesis refers to the ability of our brain to grow new neurons (even into adulthood), and neuroplasticity is the brain's ability to rewire and form new connections. Through incremental changes, it's possible to transform dysfunctional patterns of thinking and behaving into new mindsets, new memories, new skills, and new abilities. What mindsets or behaviors would you like to change? Where do you need to focus your attention this week and going forward into the weeks ahead?

Now that you've named the changes you'd like to make, what practices can you implement incrementally to rewire your brain?

# *REVIEW*

## HOW DID YOU DO THIS WEEK?

I'M FEELING:

MY FAVORITE ACTIVITY:

ONE THING I LEARNED
ABOUT MYSELF:

I GREW IN STRENGTH BY:

I GREW IN HOPE BY:

I GREW IN MEANING BY:

WEEKLY WINS:

MY FOCUS FOR INCREMENTAL GROWTH IN DAILY HABITS:

THE MOST IMPORTANT THING I DISCOVERED ABOUT
RULE THREE THIS PAST WEEK:

I'D LIKE TO GROW IN THE FOLLOWING WAY:

NEXT WEEK I WANT TO FOCUS ON:

# MONTHLY REVIEW

## HOW WELL DID YOU DO THIS MONTH?

Take time to check in with yourself to review your growth and progress. Notice how you've grown, and reflect on how you'd like to make further progress next month.

What about "embracing adversity" came naturally for you? Why?

What about "embracing adversity" did you find most difficult? Why?

Which goals or priorities were you able to meet? Are there any you would like to continue to work toward?

## Rule Three

The thing that surprised me most about myself was:

I want to improve next month by:

On a scale of 1 to 10, circle how resilient you're feeling this month.

1    2    3    4    5    6    7    8    9    10

## NOTES

This month, you are sure to become more resilient by making meaning and cultivating beauty in your life. When we don't make meaning, we are restless and experience a sense of meaninglessness, which is why making meaning matters so much. In these next few weeks, make it your intention to spend time encountering beauty, making good things, cultivating purpose, and creating meaning in your personal life. One way you may embody Rule Four is by way of space—perhaps through creating a flourishing or renewing space in your home or through encountering a space that challenges and inspires you, such as trying or returning to therapy or visiting a beautiful space. With your eyes and heart wide open, take the opportunity to participate in making good things and growing in a skill. God is always looking for us to partner with him in this creative work.

# MONTH FOUR
## RULE FOUR

# MAKE MEANING

## CULTIVATE BEAUTY

# MONTHLY CALENDAR

MONTH

| MONDAY | TUESDAY | WEDNESDAY | THURSDAY |
|--------|---------|-----------|----------|
|        |         |           |          |
|        |         |           |          |
|        |         |           |          |
|        |         |           |          |
|        |         |           |          |

*We were made for beauty and made to serve beauty.*

—REBEKAH LYONS

| FRIDAY | SATURDAY | SUNDAY |
|--------|----------|--------|
|        |          |        |
|        |          |        |
|        |          |        |
|        |          |        |
|        |          |        |

TOP PRIORITIES

RESILIENCE GOALS

# RULE FOUR | SCRIPTURES

Take time to meditate on the following Scriptures this month. They are here for you to return to as you Make Meaning.

"For I know the plans I have for you," declares the LORD, "plans to prosper you and not to harm you, plans to give you hope and a future."
—JEREMIAH 29:11

He has sent me . . .
to comfort all who mourn
    and provide for those who grieve in Zion—
to bestow on them a crown of beauty
    instead of ashes,
the oil of joy
    instead of mourning,
and a garment of praise
    instead of a spirit of despair.
They will be called oaks of righteousness,
    a planting of the LORD
    for the display of his splendor.
—ISAIAH 61:1-3

You are a chosen people, a royal priesthood, a holy nation, God's special possession, that you may declare the praises of him who called you out of darkness into his wonderful light.
—1 PETER 2:9

He has made everything beautiful in its time. He has also set eternity in the human heart; yet no one can fathom what God has done from beginning to end.
—ECCLESIASTES 3:11

The heavens declare the glory of God;
  the skies proclaim the work of his hands.
—PSALM 19:1

Many are the plans in a person's heart,
  but it is the LORD's purpose that prevails.
—PROVERBS 19:21

For we are God's handiwork, created in Christ Jesus to do good works, which God prepared in advance for us to do.
—EPHESIANS 2:10

Through [Jesus] all things were made; without him nothing was made that has been made.
—JOHN 1:3

Now may the God of peace, who through the blood of the eternal covenant brought back from the dead our Lord Jesus, that great Shepherd of the sheep, equip you with everything good for doing his will, and may he work in us what is pleasing to him, through Jesus Christ, to whom be glory for ever and ever. Amen.
—HEBREWS 13:20–21

[The LORD] satisfies the longing soul,
  and the hungry soul he fills with good things.
—PSALM 107:9 ESV

How delightful on the mountains
Are the feet of one who brings good news,
Who announces peace
And brings good news of happiness,
Who announces salvation,
And says to Zion, "Your God reigns!"

—ISAIAH 52:7 NASB

"Nothing will be impossible with God."

—LUKE 1:37 ESV

Do you see a man skillful in his work?
   He will stand before kings;
   he will not stand before obscure men.

—PROVERBS 22:29 ESV

Do not neglect your gift, which was given you through prophecy
when the body of elders laid their hands on you. Be diligent in these
matters; give yourself wholly to them, so that everyone may see
your progress.

—1 TIMOTHY 4:14–15

Whatever you do, work at it with all your heart, as working for the
Lord, not for human masters, since you know that you will receive
an inheritance from the Lord as a reward. It is the Lord Christ you
are serving.

—COLOSSIANS 3:23–24

Whatever you do, whether in word or deed, do it all in the name of
the Lord Jesus, giving thanks to God the Father through him.

—COLOSSIANS 3:17

Now to him who is able to do immeasurably more than all we
ask or imagine, according to his power that is at work within us,

to him be glory in the church and in Christ Jesus throughout all generations, for ever and ever! Amen.

—EPHESIANS 3:20-21

"Surely I am with you always, to the very end of the age."

—MATTHEW 28:20

# WEEKLY PRACTICE

*Beauty is the antidote to scarcity. When we fear, we see lack.*
*When we recognize beauty, we encounter the divine.*
—REBEKAH LYONS

## GOAL
This week I intend (purpose) to:

## INTENTION
I will take action by:

## FOCUS
My Scripture to meditate on is:

## GRATITUDE
This week I'm grateful for:

## PRACTICES
○ Start an herb garden.
○ Write a poem or song.
○ Try out a new recipe.
○ .............................................................................
○ .............................................................................

# EXAMINE

Do you tend to notice beauty or do you focus on lack? Do you find yourself being critical more than complimentary? Is your glass half empty or half full? Are you restless? Take a few minutes to examine the lens you look through. Perhaps your perspective has changed over the years. Be honest with yourself.

We all have longings. We long for something we seem to be missing. Open your heart and mind and consider what you might be longing for in this season of life.

Beneath our longing is often a desire for the presence of God where we feel he may be absent and silent. Have you tried to fill that silence with something? Write a short prayer in which you ask God to reveal the deeper desire in your heart. Thank him for meeting your every need.

RULE FOUR | WEEK ONE
# *REVIEW*

## HOW DID YOU DO THIS WEEK?

I'M FEELING:

MY FAVORITE ACTIVITY:

ONE THING I LEARNED
ABOUT MYSELF:

I GREW IN STRENGTH BY:

I GREW IN HOPE BY:

I GREW IN MEANING BY:

WEEKLY WINS:

MY FAVORITE WAY TO ENCOUNTER BEAUTY:

THE MOST IMPORTANT THING I DISCOVERED ABOUT
RULE FOUR THIS PAST WEEK:

I'D LIKE TO GROW IN THE FOLLOWING WAY:

NEXT WEEK I WANT TO FOCUS ON:

# WEEKLY PRACTICE

*A life of beauty connects you with God, and in that connection, you begin to see the world differently.*
—REBEKAH LYONS

## GOAL
This week I intend (purpose) to:

## INTENTION
I will take action by:

## FOCUS
My Scripture to meditate on is:

## GRATITUDE
This week I'm grateful for:

## PRACTICES
○ Make a candle.
○ Learn to knit, sew, or crochet.
○ Use your art supplies and make something.
○ ........................................................................................
○ ........................................................................................

# *EXAMINE*

We were made for beauty and to cultivate beauty. When we go through hard times, it's often difficult to notice beauty. Yet beauty is often the very answer to our pain. Recall a time when beauty gave you a sense of peace, hope, or clarity. Where was God in that moment?

How do you encounter beauty? What is your favorite form of beauty? Perhaps take a few moments to look around and notice beauty and then write about what you see. Make it a goal to look for beauty this week.

A life of beauty connects us with God, and in that connection, we begin to see the world differently. How does beauty make you feel connected to God? How will you be intentional about experiencing beauty and connecting with God this week?

# *REVIEW*

## HOW DID YOU DO THIS WEEK?

I'M FEELING:

MY FAVORITE ACTIVITY:

ONE THING I LEARNED
ABOUT MYSELF:

I GREW IN STRENGTH BY:

I GREW IN HOPE BY:

I GREW IN MEANING BY:

WEEKLY WINS:

A LONGING I'VE BEGUN TO NAME:

THE MOST IMPORTANT THING I DISCOVERED ABOUT
RULE FOUR THIS PAST WEEK:

I'D LIKE TO GROW IN THE FOLLOWING WAY:

NEXT WEEK I WANT TO FOCUS ON:

# WEEKLY PRACTICE

*The places we inhabit matter. They not only serve as the backdrop of our memories, but they also help form our memories and contribute to the joy we experience daily.*
—TIMOTHY D. WILLARD

## GOAL
This week I intend (purpose) to:

## INTENTION
I will take action by:

## FOCUS
My Scripture to meditate on is:

## GRATITUDE
This week I'm grateful for:

## PRACTICES
○ Declutter your home.
○ Bake something and share it with a neighbor.
○ Repair something that needs mending.
○ .............................................................................................
○ .............................................................................................

# EXAMINE

We need spaces that restore and rejuvenate us. Does your home feel like a place where your soul can find rest? If not, take some time to think about how to create that for yourself. Be creative. What do you want your home to look and feel like? What does your space need in order to embody rejuvenation? For inspiration, think of some of your favorite places to come up with ideas (hotels, restaurants, special stores, a friend's house, and the like).

Do you have any spaces right now that challenge you and build resilience? Perhaps for you it'll look like going to the gym or to therapy. Maybe it means trying something new on vacation that is outside of your comfort zone or visiting a place to which you've never been. What spaces have helped you stretch and grow? What are you feeling inspired and challenged to try— something you wouldn't have considered before?

The process of naming our desire for beauty can shift our thinking. How can you start to name the beauty you're longing for? List some ways you can slow down and look for beauty in the world around you. What spaces inspire you and bring connection for you? Where do you feel God's presence and notice him at work?

# REVIEW

## HOW DID YOU DO THIS WEEK?

I'M FEELING:

MY FAVORITE ACTIVITY:

ONE THING I LEARNED
ABOUT MYSELF:

I GREW IN STRENGTH BY:

I GREW IN HOPE BY:

I GREW IN MEANING BY:

WEEKLY WINS:

SOMETHING I CREATED OR MADE (OR PLAN TO):

THE MOST IMPORTANT THING I DISCOVERED ABOUT
RULE FOUR THIS PAST WEEK:

I'D LIKE TO GROW IN THE FOLLOWING WAY:

NEXT WEEK I WANT TO FOCUS ON:

# WEEKLY PRACTICE

*You [Lord] have made us for yourself, and our*
*heart is restless until it rests in you.*
—AUGUSTINE

## GOAL
This week I intend (purpose) to:

## INTENTION
I will take action by:

## FOCUS
My Scripture to meditate on is:

## GRATITUDE
This week I'm grateful for:

## PRACTICES
○ Volunteer for a good cause.
○ Reflect on where your talents and burdens intersect.
○ Make a space in your home beautiful.
○ ......................................................................................................
○ ......................................................................................................

# EXAMINE

Beauty isn't something we only long for or seek. Beauty is something we create. And God invites us to partner with him to create good things. Take some time to ponder how you feel about creating. What did you discover as you reflected? What things do you already know how to create?

Creating good things takes time. Often we resort to busywork, consuming and doing, because it's easy, because it's the norm. What holds you back from creating? Would you create more if you felt you had more time?

What would you like to create or learn to make? Allow yourself to imagine and dream. Perhaps you can remember back to that recipe you wanted to try, the class you thought about taking, the paint colors that caught your attention in the store, the seeds you meant to order, the craft you were ready to begin but didn't know where to start. What can you begin to create this week and who can help you? Sometimes asking for help or creating with someone else is all we need to get started.

# REVIEW

## HOW DID YOU DO THIS WEEK?

I'M FEELING:

MY FAVORITE ACTIVITY:

ONE THING I LEARNED
ABOUT MYSELF:

I GREW IN STRENGTH BY:

I GREW IN HOPE BY:

I GREW IN MEANING BY:

WEEKLY WINS:

A FLOURISHING SPACE FOR ME:

THE MOST IMPORTANT THING I DISCOVERED ABOUT
RULE FOUR THIS PAST WEEK:

I'D LIKE TO GROW IN THE FOLLOWING WAY:

NEXT WEEK I WANT TO FOCUS ON:

# MONTHLY REVIEW

## HOW WELL DID YOU DO THIS MONTH?

Take time to check in with yourself to review your growth and progress. Notice how you've grown, and reflect on how you'd like to make further progress next month.

What about "making meaning" came naturally for you? Why?

What about "making meaning" did you find most difficult? Why?

Which goals or priorities were you able to meet? Are there any you would like to continue to work toward?

## Rule Four

The thing that surprised me most about myself was:

I want to improve next month by:

On a scale of 1 to 10, circle how resilient you're feeling this month.

1    2    3    4    5    6    7    8    9    10

## NOTES

You've put in time, heart, and energy to grow in resilience, and I'm certain you're beginning to notice progress and growth! Congratulations. Let's finish the final rule—and final month—strong. To be resilient people, we need each other. Building a resilient life cannot be done alone. Living resiliently requires intention to come alongside others, embrace diversity, and enjoy the bounty of community. Rule Five asks us to be resilient people in a resilient community. This month, you'll examine what your community looks like. *Do I have a group of friends and family that I can rely on?* In the coming weeks, you'll practice building and strengthening your community by locking arms, building small and strong, and harnessing the power of "we."

MONTH FIVE
RULE FIVE

# ENDURE
# TOGETHER

## INVITE OTHERS IN

# MONTHLY CALENDAR

MONTH

| MONDAY | TUESDAY | WEDNESDAY | THURSDAY |
|--------|---------|-----------|----------|
|        |         |           |          |
|        |         |           |          |
|        |         |           |          |
|        |         |           |          |
|        |         |           |          |

> *Resilience isn't found in the power of me;*
> *resilience is formed in the power of we.*

—REBEKAH LYONS

| FRIDAY | SATURDAY | SUNDAY |
|--------|----------|--------|
|        |          |        |

**TOP PRIORITIES**

. . . . . . .
. . . . . . .
. . . . . . .
. . . . . . .
. . . . . . .

**RESILIENCE GOALS**

. . . . . . .
. . . . . . .
. . . . . . .
. . . . . . .
. . . . . . .

# RULE FIVE | SCRIPTURES

Take time to meditate on the following Scriptures this month. They are here for you to return to as you Endure Together.

"The kingdom of heaven is like a mustard seed, which a man took and planted in his field. Though it is the smallest of all seeds, yet when it grows, it is the largest of garden plants and becomes a tree, so that the birds come and perch in its branches."
—MATTHEW 13:31-32

"The kingdom of heaven is like yeast that a woman took and mixed into about sixty pounds of flour until it worked all through the dough."
—MATTHEW 13:33

Therefore confess your sins to each other and pray for each other so that you may be healed. The prayer of a righteous person is powerful and effective.
—JAMES 5:16

As iron sharpens iron,
    so one person sharpens another.
—PROVERBS 27:17

The righteous will flourish like a palm tree,
    they will grow like a cedar of Lebanon;
planted in the house of the LORD,
    they will flourish in the courts of our God.
—PSALM 92:12-13

GROWTH

"My prayer is not for them alone. I pray also for those who will believe in me through their message, that all of them may be one, Father, just as you are in me and I am in you. May they also be in us so that the world may believe that you have sent me. I have given them the glory that you gave me, that they may be one as we are one—I in them and you in me—so that they may be brought to complete unity. Then the world will know that you sent me and have loved them even as you have loved me."

—JOHN 17:20-23

All the believers were together and had everything in common.

—ACTS 2:44

UNITY

So in Christ we, though many, form one body, and each member belongs to all the others.

—ROMANS 12:5

If we walk in the light, as he is in the light, we have fellowship with one another, and the blood of Jesus, his Son, purifies us from all sin.

—1 JOHN 1:7

"For where two or three gather in my name, there am I with them."

—MATTHEW 18:20

How good and pleasant it is
    when God's people live together in unity!

—PSALM 133:1

Carry each other's burdens, and in this way you will fulfill the law of Christ.

—GALATIANS 6:2

A friend loves at all times,
and a brother is born for a time of adversity.

—PROVERBS 17:17

"My command is this: Love each other as I have loved you. Greater love has no one than this: to lay down one's life for one's friends."

—JOHN 15:12–13

Do nothing out of selfish ambition or vain conceit. Rather, in humility value others above yourselves, not looking to your own interests but each of you to the interests of the others.

—PHILIPPIANS 2:3–4

"Now that I, your Lord and Teacher, have washed your feet, you also should wash one another's feet."

—JOHN 13:14

Do not use your freedom to indulge the flesh; rather, serve one another humbly in love. For the entire law is fulfilled in keeping this one command: "Love your neighbor as yourself."

—GALATIANS 5:13–14

"They triumphed over him
by the blood of the Lamb
and by the word of their testimony."

—REVELATION 12:11

"Wake up, sleeper,
rise from the dead,
and Christ will shine on you."

—EPHESIANS 5:14

Bear with each other and forgive one another if any of you has a grievance against someone. Forgive as the Lord forgave you.

—COLOSSIANS 3:13

He who began a good work in you will carry it on to completion until the day of Christ Jesus.

—PHILIPPIANS 1:6

Let us hold unswervingly to the hope we profess, for he who promised is faithful.

—HEBREWS 10:23

Blessed is the one who perseveres under trial because, having stood the test, that person will receive the crown of life that the Lord has promised to those who love him.

—JAMES 1:12

# WEEKLY PRACTICE

*A resilient culture means grabbing hands and leaping together, knowing that the leaping will go better because you're not alone.*
—MIKE ERWIN

## GOAL
This week I intend (purpose) to:

## INTENTION
I will take action by:

## FOCUS
My Scripture to meditate on is:

## GRATITUDE
This week I'm grateful for:

## PRACTICES
○ Take a walk with a friend.
○ Call a long-distance friend.
○ Invite a family member or friend over for a meal.
○ ......................................................................................................................
○ ......................................................................................................................

RULE FIVE | WEEK ONE

# EXAMINE

Take time to reflect on the concept of community. Do you feel as though you have community in your life? Is it something you've been longing for? Have you ever been part of a community—a place where you truly felt you belonged and had purpose? What does living in community look like to you?

Who in your life is part of your community? Who could you potentially begin to build community with? Bring to mind family members, friends, neighbors, fellow parents, or church members—those who share a common goal.

This week, how will you begin to, intentionally and incrementally, build and participate in community? Take time to think through ideas and list actionable steps.

# REVIEW

## HOW DID YOU DO THIS WEEK?

I'M FEELING:

MY FAVORITE ACTIVITY:

ONE THING I LEARNED
ABOUT MYSELF:

I GREW IN STRENGTH BY:

I GREW IN HOPE BY:

I GREW IN MEANING BY:

WEEKLY WINS:

I PARTICIPATED IN/BUILT COMMUNITY BY:

THE MOST IMPORTANT THING I DISCOVERED ABOUT
RULE FIVE THIS PAST WEEK:

I'D LIKE TO GROW IN THE FOLLOWING WAY:

NEXT WEEK I WANT TO FOCUS ON:

# WEEKLY PRACTICE

*Resilience grows with common commitment.*
—REBEKAH LYONS

## GOAL
This week I intend (purpose) to:

## INTENTION
I will take action by:

## FOCUS
My Scripture to meditate on is:

## GRATITUDE
This week I'm grateful for:

## PRACTICES
- ○ Volunteer at your church or for an organization.
- ○ Send a card or letter of encouragement.
- ○ Start or join a community Bible study.
- ○ ......................................................................................................
- ○ ......................................................................................................

# EXAMINE

Studies have shown that when we build connections with like-minded people through empathy and understanding, we bolster our resilience. During difficult times, do you tend to isolate yourself or do you choose to lean into community? Why do you think that is?

Crisis offers us the opportunity to not only recover but to grow stronger and more resilient. Think of a time when you faced a difficult situation or crisis, whether it was a personal or corporate experience. As you look back, although the circumstance was difficult, in what ways can you see strength and growth in yourself?

Think about and describe the type of community you need, are longing for, and desire to build. Do you need a Bible study, a group for moms, a regularly scheduled gathering of neighbors?

# REVIEW

## HOW DID YOU DO THIS WEEK?

I'M FEELING:

MY FAVORITE ACTIVITY:

ONE THING I LEARNED
ABOUT MYSELF:

I GREW IN STRENGTH BY:

I GREW IN HOPE BY:

I GREW IN MEANING BY:

WEEKLY WINS:

I MET SOMEONE'S NEED BY:

THE MOST IMPORTANT THING I DISCOVERED ABOUT
RULE FIVE THIS PAST WEEK:

I'D LIKE TO GROW IN THE FOLLOWING WAY:

NEXT WEEK I WANT TO FOCUS ON:

# WEEKLY PRACTICE

*Though she be but little, she is fierce.*
—WILLIAM SHAKESPEARE

## GOAL
This week I intend (purpose) to:

## INTENTION
I will take action by:

## FOCUS
My Scripture to meditate on is:

## GRATITUDE
This week I'm grateful for:

## PRACTICES
◯ Initiate a vulnerable conversation.
◯ Pray with someone in need.
◯ Apologize to someone and forgive them.
◯ ......................................................................
◯ ......................................................................

# EXAMINE

The world we live in has conditioned us to believe that "more" is better. However, "more" is not always sustainable. In what ways have you bought into this mindset?

With God, size does not equal strength. Take a moment to read the parable in Matthew 13:31–32 of the mustard seed. Does Jesus' teaching here remind you of what God can do, even with what we think is very little? God can take the smallest things and use them to change the world. He took a small band of followers who set into motion the community we know today to be the church of Christ worldwide. What might God be asking you and your community to do with the small things he has given you?

Take time to think about the people in your community. Is there anyone currently in need? How can you tangibly offer help and also rally others to come alongside and bear the burden?

# REVIEW

## HOW DID YOU DO THIS WEEK?

I'M FEELING:

MY FAVORITE ACTIVITY:

ONE THING I LEARNED
ABOUT MYSELF:

I GREW IN STRENGTH BY:

I GREW IN HOPE BY:

I GREW IN MEANING BY:

WEEKLY WINS:

ONE THING I CAN OFFER MY COMMUNITY:

THE MOST IMPORTANT THING I DISCOVERED ABOUT
RULE FIVE THIS PAST WEEK:

I'D LIKE TO GROW IN THE FOLLOWING WAY:

NEXT WEEK I WANT TO FOCUS ON:

# WEEKLY PRACTICE

*Resilient lives are not formed in isolation;*
*resilient lives are forged in community.*
—REBEKAH LYONS

## GOAL
This week I intend (purpose) to:

## INTENTION
I will take action by:

## FOCUS
My Scripture to meditate on is:

## GRATITUDE
This week I'm grateful for:

## PRACTICES
- ◯ Text a Scripture to a friend in need.
- ◯ Meet a tangible need (e.g., help clean someone's home, cook a meal).
- ◯ Share one or two prayer requests you have.
- ◯ .................................................................................
- ◯ .................................................................................

# *EXAMINE*

As you create intention and begin to build community, in what ways can you continue to grow away from a life of isolation and toward one of community? In what ways can you reach out to someone who is feeling isolated?

Christ-centered community reminds us of who we really are and also keeps us accountable. What do you need to be reminded of today? Is there anything for which you need accountability? In turn, how can you remind someone else who they truly are? How can you offer accountability?

Are there any ways in which comfort and complacency might be betraying your deepest longings? How do you need to challenge yourself for continued growth and the building of resilience?

# REVIEW

## HOW DID YOU DO THIS WEEK?

I'M FEELING:

MY FAVORITE ACTIVITY:

ONE THING I LEARNED
ABOUT MYSELF:

I GREW IN STRENGTH BY:

I GREW IN HOPE BY:

I GREW IN MEANING BY:

WEEKLY WINS:

I'D LIKE TO INVITE THE FOLLOWING PEOPLE INTO
COMMUNITY:

THE MOST IMPORTANT THING I DISCOVERED ABOUT
RULE FIVE THIS PAST WEEK:

I'D LIKE TO GROW IN THE FOLLOWING WAY:

NEXT WEEK I WANT TO FOCUS ON:

# MONTHLY REVIEW

## HOW WELL DID YOU DO THIS MONTH?

Take time to check in with yourself to review your growth and progress. Notice how you've grown, as well as how you might like to make further progress next month.

What about "enduring together" came naturally for you? Why?

What about "enduring together" did you find most difficult? Why?

Which goals or priorities were you able to meet? Are there any you would like to continue to work toward?

## Rule Five

The thing that surprised me most about myself was:

I want to improve next month by:

On a scale of 1 to 10, circle how resilient you're feeling this month.

1     2     3     4     5     6     7     8     9     10

## NOTES

# RESILIENCE REVIEW

Great work. Are you feeling more resilient? You've worked hard to build a resilient life filled with strength, hope, and meaning. Now is the time to reflect on and celebrate your overall growth and progress.

## RULE ONE: NAME THE PAIN
I experienced growth by:

I want to continue to build my resilience in this area by:

A memorable way I named the pain and became honest was:

## RULE TWO: SHIFT THE NARRATIVE
I experienced growth by:

I want to continue to build my resilience in this area by:

A memorable way I shifted the narrative and renewed my mind was:

## RULE THREE: EMBRACE ADVERSITY
I experienced growth by:

I want to continue to build my resilience in this area by:

A memorable way I embraced adversity and trained with resistance was:

## RULE FOUR: MAKE MEANING

I experienced growth by:

I want to continue to build my resilience in this area by:

A memorable way I made meaning and cultivated beauty was:

## RULE FIVE: ENDURE TOGETHER

I experienced growth by:

I want to continue to build my resilience in this area by:

A memorable way I endured together and invited others in was:

On a scale of 1 to 10, circle how effective you were with each rule.

Rule One    1   2   3   4   5   6   7   8   9   10

Rule Two    1   2   3   4   5   6   7   8   9   10

Rule Three   1   2   3   4   5   6   7   8   9   10

Rule Four   1   2   3   4   5   6   7   8   9   10

Rule Five   1   2   3   4   5   6   7   8   9   10

# RESOURCES

## JOIN THE WELLNESS JOURNEY
Continue to build your resilience with the following:

## FREE RESOURCES AT WWW.REBEKAHLYONS.COM

**Tech Detox Guide:** https://rebekahlyons.com/techdetox

**30 Verses for Anxiety:** https://rebekahlyons.com/anxiety

**Take Inventory Guide:** https://rebekahlyons.com/takeinventory

**Fighting Fear Guide:** https://rebekahlyons.com/fightingfear

**Strength & Dignity Study:** https://www.rebekahlyons.com/strength

**10 Tips for Mental Health:** https://rebekahlyons.com/mentalhealth

**A Three-Week Study on Confidence:** https://www.rebekahlyons.com/confidence

**A Ten-Day Video Study on Rest:** https://rebekahlyons.com/rest

**A Six-Week Video Study on Freedom:** https://rebekahlyons.com/freedom

**Healthiest Rhythm Quiz:** https://rebekahlyons.com/quiz

**Weekly Rhythm Guide:** https://www.rebekahlyons.com/rhythmguide

**3 Ways to Overcome Loneliness Webinar:** https://rebekahlyons.com/replay

**Live Free Conversation Guide:** https://rebekahlyons.com/livefree

**Emotional Health Series:** https://rebekahlyons.com/emotionalhealth

## CHAPTER DOWNLOADS

**Embracing Your Calling:** https://rebekahlyons.com/calling

**Take a Walk:** https://rebekahlyons.com/takeawalk

**Morning Routine:** https://rebekahlyons.com/morningroutine

**Free to Grieve:** https://rebekahlyons.com/grief

**Free to Rest:** https://rebekahlyons.com/free-to-rest

**Permission to Play:** https://rebekahlyons.com/play

## RETREATS: RebekahLyons.com/retreats

**Rhythms Retreat:** https://rebekahlyons.com/rhythmsretreat

**Emotional Health Retreat:** https://rebekahlyons.com/ehretreat